THE FINAL RIP-OFF:

REVERSE MORTGAGES

Arthur Paul Ernst

Edited by Robert W. Pladek

Fiduciary Press LLC

Princeton, NJ

Edited by Robert W. Pladek, Esq.

Published in the United States of America

Fiduciary Press, LLC
P.O. Box 1356
Princeton, NJ 08542

Visit us online at:
www.fiduciarypress.com

Second Edition: November 2018

ISBN 978-0-9974185-4-5

Preface

It is hard to get through an hour of commercial television without seeing a celebrity promote reverse mortgages as means to a better life for seniors. Far from life enhancing, these costly financial scams destroy wealth, providing gullible victims with modest cash amounts as vastly more home equity is unwittingly taken by the lender.

If used to get funds for only a short spell, reverse mortgages are more usurious than famously egregious credit card cash advances. If used to get cash for an extended period, a reverse mortgage is basically a contract through which a home is sold for a fraction of its market value.

Since the first edition of this book was written, the U.S. Department of Housing and Urban Development established new factors and fee levels. For the most relevant range of interest rates and ages the new regulations reduced the cash available to borrowers as a percentage of home value. Meanwhile the mortgage insurance premium charged at closing was quadrupled for all term and tenure loans. Reverse mortgages were already financially harmful; they got worse.

Reverse mortgages are sold as a late life resource. They are only available to people at least 62 years of age, often retired with no new means of income. Banks use reverse mortgages to latch onto the only substantial and marketable asset seniors generally own. They do not want the home; they want the proceeds from the loan's ultimate payoff. Given the lien on the home, a payoff and outsized profit are secured upon closing. The magnitude of profit for the bank and financial deterioration for the borrower are merely a function of time and borrowing pattern.

Barring a windfall such as a lottery win, victims will not be able to raise new funds to pay off a reverse mortgage. When a borrower sells the home and pays off the accumulated charges, it is likely that the net amount received – if indeed anything is received – will not be adequate to fund a new home. In the best of circumstances – a long life and maximized, though still paltry cash advances – 95% of the home's value will go to the bank after the death of the borrower; net of transaction costs nothing will be left for heirs.

In either case, for the victim a reverse mortgage will have served as the final rip-off.

Table of Contents

Section I

What Is a Reverse Mortgage

1: Introduction

Contrary to statements in many ads, reverse mortgages:

- do not provide any income.
- bring on new ways a home can be seized.
- effectively result in the sale of a home for a fraction of its fair price.

Additionally, reverse mortgages:

- entail costs higher than the worst credit cards.
- provide zero tax benefit – unlike conventional mortgages.
- wipe out late life savings; often entire estates.

Reverse mortgages are callously aimed at vulnerable seniors struggling to make ends meet. These people should be helped, not fleeced.

Indeed, seniors are conned through cleverly scripted ads featuring well-known actors whose familiarity induces trust. This trust is horribly misplaced as viewers are goaded to grab some easy cash while blindly handing the bank vastly more in terms of home equity.

There are prudent options for homeowners seeking financial security and better cash flow. Many reverse mortgage 'counselors' mean well but are themselves fooled by misleading information provided by lenders and their hired marketing 'research' associates. For every situation or goal mentioned in a reverse mortgage ad or brochure, there is a better solution.

This book was written to help the unwary and the tempted. The effects of reverse mortgage charges are isolated, clarified, and highlighted without the obfuscation found in lender propaganda. No rational person who fully understands a reverse mortgage would ever get one.

2: How a Reverse Mortgage Works

A reverse mortgage, officially termed a home equity conversion mortgage (HECM), is a loan through which a bank puts a lien on your home and lends you money via cash advances. To set up the arrangement, fees are charged up front. Each time you borrow more money, fees are billed. Daily, interest and mortgage insurance are charged on the growing balance.

A borrower does not have to make any payments on a reverse mortgage as long as he or she lives in the house, pays property taxes, maintains it, and insures it at levels the bank requires. But the loan must be paid off at some point. Barring a lottery win or similar windfall, such usually occurs upon the sale of the home; perhaps when the borrower moves, or after a borrower dies, or upon foreclosure.

How do you get money?

Abiding within the confines of the U.S. Department of Housing and Urban Development (H.U.D.), you have three basic choices for receiving cash flow: a lump sum; monthly payments for life (tenure); and monthly payments for a defined period (term). In all three cases, including an implied case in which no money is borrowed right away, you can also have access to a line of credit for additional funds if such are available.

How much can you get?

For all three cash flow options, there is a maximum allowable loan balance which is a function of your age, the loan interest rate, and your home value. H.U.D. provides a table of factors which pertain to every combination of age and interest rate. A broad sampling of these factors can be found in Appendix D.

To illustrate, if you are 65 and the loan interest rate is 5%, cross-referencing those facts in the H.U.D. table reveals a factor of 43%. This percentage is the maximum fraction of your home's value that you can be approved for. If your home is valued at $300,000, you can, at most, be approved for an opening reverse mortgage balance of $129,000. The amount you can receive is actually less. Closing costs and fees will reduce your net cash flow. So too will potential set-asides – amounts the bank can keep separate for future payment of insurance, property taxes, and/or maintenance.

For the lump sum option, the amount you can receive is pretty straight forward as the funds come right away per the calculation just described. For the term and tenure options, the calculated maximum refers to the present value of those future monthly payments. Examples of all three options are detailed in Appendices A, B and C.

What are the costs?

Before you get one penny, closing costs apply. You will be charged 2% of the appraised value of your home for the initial mortgage insurance premium. You will also be charged an origination fee of 2% of the first $200,000 of home value plus 1% of the next $200,000. Note that these percentages are based on home value, unlike and vastly worse than regular mortgages which base fees on the loan amount. But like a regular mortgage, you will also be charged for appraisal, title search, recording fees, and other incidentals. For a $300,000 home, the mortgage insurance would be $6,000, the origination fee $5,000, and a reasonable estimate of other costs would be $2,500, for total closing costs of $13,500.

Going forward, you will be charged interest plus continuing mortgage insurance of 0.5% on the outstanding balance. If you receive monthly payments via the term or tenure payment options, the bank is allowed to charge you as much as $30 per payment.

As for the rate of interest, reverse mortgages generally charge more than conventional mortgages. The rate of interest is locked in only if you take a lump sum payment and receive no further money after the first year. In all other situations the interest rate will be variable.

What is the actual cash flow?

Appendices A, B, and C provide detailed examples of reverse mortgage loans using lump sum, term, and tenure options. Chapter 13 adds another example with home appreciation. For a brief understanding, here is a summary of what occurs. Assume circumstances just outlined: you are 65, your home is appraised at $300,000, you have no other liens on the home, the interest rate is 5%, and total closing costs are $13,500.

Lump sum

On day one, closing, the account is opened and closing costs of $13,500 are charged. Your balance can at most be $129,000, so after subtracting closing costs you receive $115,500. But you now owe $129,000.

After one year you will owe $136,277, indicating a cost of $21,277. After ten years you will owe $223,309, or almost double what you received. If in year 15 you decide to sell your home or it passes to your kids, a balance of $293,808 will have to be paid. Appendix A shows the flows and impact on wealth in more detail.

Monthly payments

Using H.U.D. guidelines, monthly payments of about $795 for 20 years would equate to a present value of $129,000 minus closing costs. Similar to the lump sum case, on day one closing costs of $13,500 are charged. Thus on day one you would receive $795. You would owe $14,295.

Going forward you would receive about $795 per month. After one year you will have received $9,534; you will owe $24,347. After ten years you will have received $95,341; you will owe $154,088. If in year 15 you sell your home or pass it to your kids, a balance of $259,182 will have to be paid – compared to total cash received of $143,011. Appendices B and C show detailed examples of term and tenure options.

Recapping, the reverse mortgage is so named because payments go from the bank to you, versus regular mortgages in which money goes from you to the bank. Also, while the amount you owe drops over time with a regular mortgage, with a reverse mortgage the amount you owe goes up – very dramatically.

Lenders and their pitchmen deceptively boast that reverse mortgages allow homeowners to use home equity. The fact is: reverse mortgages don't allow you to use your equity; they cause you to lose most of it.

Like credit card cash advances, reverse mortgage payments provide temporary cash flow but they damage your financial condition. Just how badly they do such is examined through the rest of this book.

3: A Reverse Mortgage Provides No Income

Many institutions and counselors use the word income when referring to the cash flow from reverse mortgages. Such phrasing is an outright lie.

If you put a credit card into an ATM and get cash, did your income just rise by the amount you took out? Of course not! In fact if you paid a fee to get cash, your expenses went up by that fee while income was unchanged. Your net income actually went down.

Reverse mortgage payments are like credit card cash advances on steroids. When you receive money through a reverse mortgage, you are borrowing money. Nothing has been earned. The amount you owe grows every time you receive money, and it grows at an increasing rate daily as interest and mortgage insurance are charged on an ever-growing balance.

For example, assume circumstances described in Appendix C. You are 65, own a $300,000 home debt-free, and you decide to get a monthly stream of cash for life via a reverse mortgage. Upon receipt of your first $620, you would owe the bank $14,120: the first payment plus $13,500 closing costs. During the first year you would receive cash totaling $7,443. Meanwhile your mortgage balance will grow to $22,203.

Figure 3-1: Reverse Mortgage Damage to Net Income

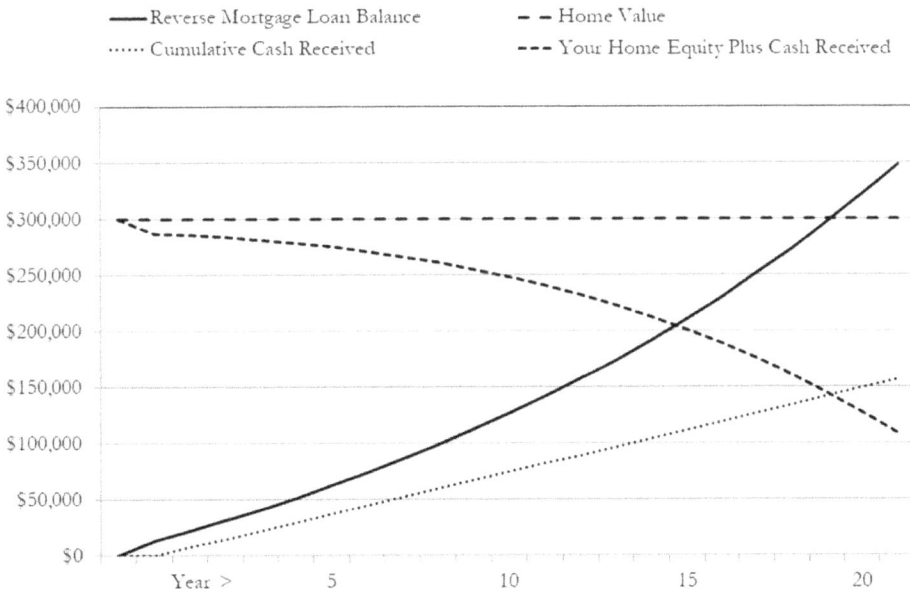

Your income did not go up. Net, your income for this one year dropped by $14,760! But income was indeed generated...for the bank and the rep who 'helped' you. If you continue apace, by the end of year five your net income will have plummeted by $24,992. As of year ten, your loss will hit $51,862. You will have received $74,430 by then, but you will owe the bank $126,292. Your finances will keep deteriorating at an increasing pace as long as you have the reverse mortgage.

4: New Ways for Your Home to Be Seized

If you own your home without a mortgage, other than failure to pay property taxes there is practically no means for someone to seize your home. If you get a reverse mortgage, there are additional ways you can lose your home. As mentioned elsewhere, the bank does not want your home; it wants the proceeds from the sale of your home.

Figure 4-1: Foreclosure Triggers

	No Mortgage	Regular Mortgage	Reverse Mortgage
Fail to Pay Property Tax	X	X	X
Fail to Pay Mortgage		X	
Fail to Insure			X
Fail to Maintain Property			X
Live Elsewhere for 1 Year			X

Reverse mortgages usually contain clauses demanding a certain level of maintenance for your property. If the financial institution deems you are not keeping things up to its satisfaction, it can take your home.

If you do not purchase property insurance at the level the bank requires, again your home can be lost.

If you live elsewhere for as little as a year – perhaps to help raise a grandchild, or maybe for needed hospice care – your home can be seized while you are away.

Again, the bank does not want your home. It wants to collect all the interest, fees, and equity you contractually forfeited. Your home's sale allows this to happen.

At the time you might secure a reverse mortgage the scenarios above may seem improbable. But things change. Health declines. Prices go up; taxes too. If payments from a reverse mortgage are needed to meet your current expenses, what happens over the course of time as taxes, insurance, maintenance, and all other costs rise?

To avert such home seizures, banks can require "set-asides". These are separate accounts where your money is parked to cover future property taxes, insurance, and/or maintenance. This sounds benign, but it is the opposite. The bank is using your money to protect its profit. Money put into set-asides reduces the amount of cash you receive. The cost of borrowing through a reverse mortgage is already atrociously high. With set-asides, the cost is astronomical.

5: Usurious Short-Term Costs

Ads for reverse mortgages promote their use for short-term needs such as filling holes in the budget, improving your home, and paying off debt. You shed palpable financial burdens while taking on reverse mortgage costs that feel painless because they are simply added to the amount owed. But the costs are real and vastly worse than famously egregious credit cards.

Figure 5-1: Reverse Mortgage vs. Credit Card Cash Advances

—— Reverse Mortgage Loan Balance   – – Credit Card Advance Balance   --- Cash Received

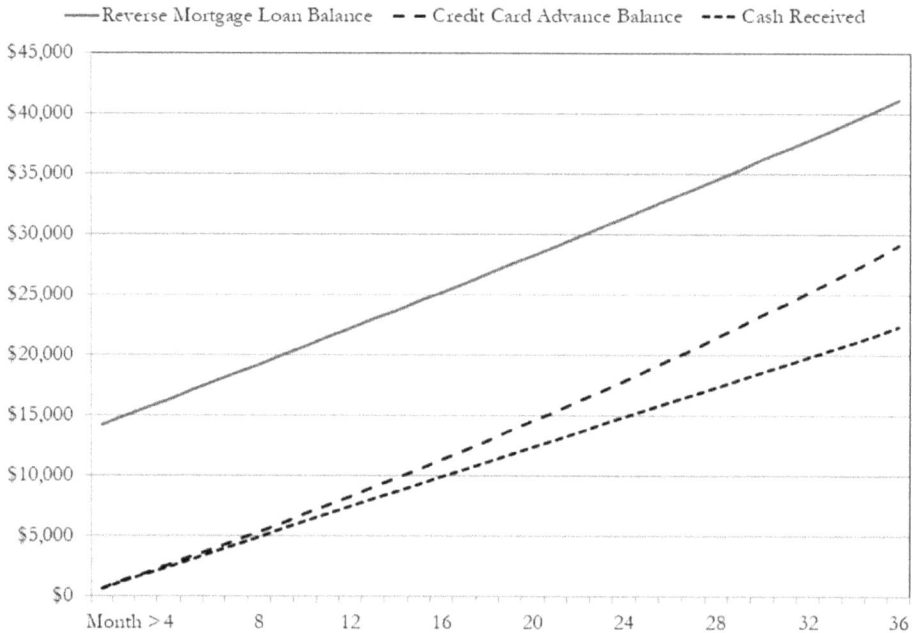

Assume you need cash for just a few years and consider a tenure reverse mortgage as modeled in Appendix C. You use your $300,000 home to secure monthly cash flow of $620.

With closing costs of $13,500, interest of 5%, mortgage insurance of 0.5%, and a monthly payment fee of $25, after receiving $7,443 during the first year you would owe $22,203. If you paid this off right after receiving your 12th payment, your effective annualized cost of borrowing will have been over 600%. If you instead take payments for another year, you will have received $14,886 and owe $31,396. Paying off the loan after your 24th payment will render an annualized cost of borrowing of roughly 100%. These effective rates are more like the vig demanded by loan sharks than charges one would expect from a legitimate financial institution.

By comparison, assume you attain the same cash flow through the terrible route of credit card cash advances. With an upfront fee of 4% for such advances, each time you get $620 you would add $645 to your balance.

Your balance would daily be charged interest; here let's assume an annual 15% rate. After the first year, you will have received the same $7,443 obtained with the reverse mortgage. Your card balance would be $8,296 – bad, but almost $14,000 better than the reverse mortgage. After two years and receipt of $14,886 you would owe the credit card issuer $17,925; again quite awful, but still far less than the reverse mortgage – over $13,000 less.

You would never use cash advances in this manner for a period of years. Most likely you would pay off any credit card balance in a fairly short spell. The fact that reverse mortgages are even worse says much.

Despite the usurious costs, a reverse mortgage rep might highlight the 'benefit' of not having to make any payments. But as time passes, the loan balance would continue to balloon. This ballooning of the balance highlights a lethal feature that reverse mortgages have and credit cards do not; a lien.

If you have a credit card balance and fall into dire straits, the lender can only sue and settle. With a reverse mortgage, the lender controls your home. Even if it means foreclosure, the bank will collect all of the cash it gave you plus all fees and interest.

A credit card puts the bank at risk. A reverse mortgage takes risk away from the bank and puts all potential and actual financial harm squarely on you. Of course, a competent financial counselor would advise you to stay out of high cost short-term debt altogether.

6: Long-Term Result Is a Fire Sale of Your Home

The maximum amount of money you can receive via a reverse mortgage is some fraction of your home's worth. Depending on interest rates a 62-year old might get between 18.5% and 52.6% of the home's value, minus closing costs. An 80-year old might get between 34.2% and 61%, again minus closing costs.

Because of the closing costs, early repayment of a reverse mortgage is quite punitive in terms of the annualized cost of funds. As time passes and the amount owed grows, repayment becomes less and less likely. Barring a windfall such as a lottery win or a substantial inheritance, in the long run there is a great likelihood that the money received through a reverse mortgage will be the only compensation you ever get for your home.

For instance, assume circumstances outlined in Appendices A, B, and C. At age 65, with a $300,000 home and 5% interest, through a reverse mortgage you could receive about $115,500 net of closing costs, or $795 per month for 20 years, or $620 per month for life.

Figure 6-1: Cash Received vs. Bank Ownership of Your Home

	Lump Sum Reverse Mortgage	Tenure Reverse Mortgage	Term Reverse Mortgage
Amount Owed at End of Year 1	$136,277	$22,203	$24,347
Cash Received by End of Year 1	$115,500	$7,443	$9,534
Amount Owed at End of Year 10	$223,309	$126,292	$154,088
Cash Received by End of Year 10	$115,500	$74,430	$95,341
Year Loan Balance Passes $300,000 Home Value	16	20	17
Cash Received by Time Loan Balance Passes $300,000	$115,500	$142,365	$158,432

In all three cases, the reverse mortgage balance will grow to an amount that exceeds the appraised home value in less than 20 years. For the lump sum, tenure and term options, the loan passes $300,000 in the 16th, 20th, and 17th year respectively. Meanwhile the amounts received by then total $115,500, $142,365, and $158,432, respectively. In present value terms, at most you only get $115,500 whichever route you choose.

H.U.D. guidelines restrict a bank's claim on home equity to 95% of home value; but transaction costs – whether a new mortgage or sale of the home – usually exceed 5% of home value. Thus once enough time passes, whether your home is sold by you or handled by your estate, no one in your family will get another penny for your home beyond the reverse mortgage cash advances. Appreciation will not help; see Chapter 13.

Indirectly, H.U.D. shows you how much you would be short-changed dumping your home equity through a reverse mortgage. H.U.D. tables display the maximum percentage of your home's value you can receive in present value terms. Appendix D shows a sampling of these percentages. Referring to the chart, at 5% interest, a 62-year-old could qualify for a loan worth 41% of the home value. After closing costs, only 37% or so would be received. In the long run, the amount owed will grow from 41% of home value to effectively (after transaction costs) 100% of its value. Fully 63% of the home equity will have been forfeited to the lender; a fire sale discount.

Section II

Promoted Uses (and Harm) of Reverse Mortgages

7: Given Any Goal, They Make Things Worse

Firms trying to convince you into getting a reverse mortgage suggest assorted reasons to do so. Without bringing up consequences or costs, ads and brochures highlight the wonders of being able to stop mortgage payments, make ends meet, travel, improve the home, and more.

In effect, the products being promoted are the uses of the money. But the product actually being sold is the reverse mortgage. In every case, a reverse mortgage will make your financial situation devastatingly worse.

Any focus on the effect of the product, the reverse mortgage, would more than wipe out the teasingly promoted benefits. Knowing this, banks and reps purposely divert. It is similar to the old cigarette ads that highlighted flavor and style while avoiding topics like cancer and emphysema.

Since the ads and counselors pushing these loans will not do such, the following chapters discuss the full impact of using a reverse mortgage to achieve some of the more frequently mentioned "benefits". Alternative courses are suggested. As with credit card debt and other vehicles financial firms promote to get you to spend beyond your means, the alternative course is often a simple "don't do it".

8: Don't Get One to Pay Off Existing Debt

Some firms promote the use of a reverse mortgage to pay off an existing regular mortgage. Right away, you worsen your finances as closing costs and higher, non-deductible interest hit. Worse, instead of continuing on a path of reducing debt, lowering expense, and increasing net worth, the reverse mortgage puts you on a path of ever-increasing debt, growing expense, and declining net worth. Because you are no longer writing checks you do not notice the harm of the costly new arrangement.

For example, assume you still owe $100,000 on a mortgage with ten years remaining and a 3.5% interest rate. Your monthly payments would be about $989. To get rid of these payments, you consider getting a lump sum reverse mortgage as modeled in Appendix A; 5% interest, 0.5% continuing mortgage insurance, and closing costs of $13,500 on your $300,000 home. To pay off the $100,000 regular mortgage balance you thereby borrow $113,500 – the payoff amount plus closing costs.

Figure 8-1: After-Tax Cost of Regular and Reverse Mortgage
$100,000 balance, 10 years remaining

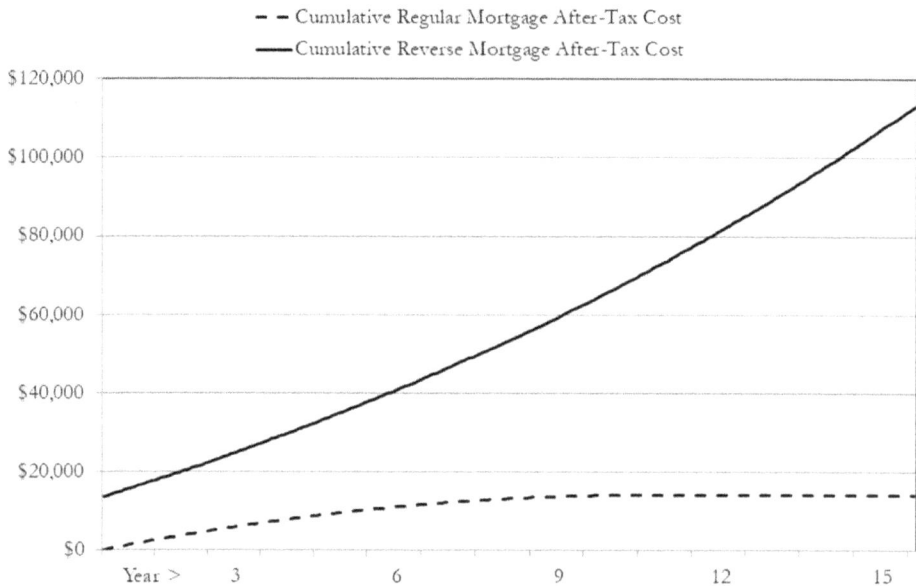

During the next two years, your regular mortgage would require about $23,733 in cash payments. Of this amount, $6,427 is interest and $17,306 is principal. This latter amount remains a part of your wealth as it reduces your mortgage balance to $82,694. Meanwhile, if a marginal tax rate of 25% is assumed, $1,607 of the $6,427 interest expense comes back to you through tax savings. Thus, the net cost of your regular mortgage would be about $4,820.

With a reverse mortgage, your balance would grow to $126,666 in those same two years. There is no tax benefit since interest is not paid; it is merely accrued and added to your account. You save about $22,126 in after-tax cash flow, but those cash savings cost you almost $44,000 in home equity – the extra $26,666 you owe plus the $17,306 you would have paid off had you stayed the course with your regular mortgage. It gets worse.

After five years, the regular mortgage would have an after-tax cost of about $10,267; the reverse mortgage cost would approach $50,000. In ten years, the regular mortgage cost peaks at just under $14,000. At that time you would own your home free and clear. With the reverse mortgage, at that same time your loan cost nears $100,000 and you would owe the bank close to $200,000.

Figure 8-2: Comparable Mortgage Costs

After:	Cumulative Regular Mortgage Interest	Cumulative Regular Mortgage After-Tax Cost	Cumulative Reverse Mortgage Cost
2 Years	$6,427	$4,820	$26,666
5 Years	$13,689	$10,267	$49,332
10 Years	$18,663	$13,997	$96,477
15 Years	$18,663	$13,997	$158,506

To make the comparison more concrete, what happens when you sell your home, or pass it to your heirs? For simplicity assume no transaction costs or appreciation. After ten years, had you kept paying your regular mortgage you would own your home debt free. Selling it at this time would reap all $300,000 of its value. If instead you refinanced with the reverse mortgage, upon the sale of your home you would have to pay a loan balance of about $196,477, leaving you with $103,523. Taking into account your mortgage payments, which required after-tax outflows of $113,997, the reverse mortgage worsened your financial situation by $82,479.

Going forward, it gets tragic. After 15 years, had you stuck with your regular mortgage, you would have made no further payments for five years and, of course, still owned all of your $300,000 home. If you refinanced via the reverse mortgage, the loan balance would climb to $273,088. Selling your home would net less than $27,000.

In the long run, there is great likelihood that refinancing a conventional mortgage with a reverse mortgage will result in the effective loss of all of your home equity; a delayed sale in which the refinanced amount is what you accepted in exchange for your entire home.

Figure 8-3: Mortgage Impact on Home Equity

	Regular Mortgage Balance	Home Equity with Regular Mortgage	Reverse Mortgage Balance	Home Equity with Reverse Mortgage
At Closing	$100,000	$200,000	$113,500	$186,500
After: 2 Years	$82,694	$217,306	$126,666	$173,334
5 Years	$54,358	$245,642	$149,332	$150,668
10 Years	$0	$300,000	$196,477	$103,523
15 Years	$0	$300,000	$273,088	$26,912

What you should do instead

Keep paying your regular mortgage; and thus keep improving your financial condition. If you cannot, you have a budget gap. This is addressed in the next chapter.

9: Don't Get One to Fill Budget Gaps

A seemingly rational excuse to get a reverse mortgage is to maintain your standard of living; to stem negative cash flow. In this situation, a reverse mortgage is not a solution. It accelerates your financial deterioration.

First, even though you receive cash, the fees and interest charged through a reverse mortgage add vastly more in expense. If you cannot afford your current cost of living, adding many thousands of dollars, perhaps hundreds of thousands cumulatively, in bank charges is not going to help.

Second, costs will probably keep going up faster than income. While a reverse mortgage might plug a gap in current cash flow, over time normal economic trends will create another gap at some point in the future. By delaying a proper budgetary move that would correct your current hole, a reverse mortgage would force you into an inevitable financial chasm.

For example, assume your monthly income is $4,500 but your monthly expenses are running at $5,000 and growing by 2% annually. To close the gap you consider a reverse mortgage as outlined in Appendix C. To help make the analysis more concrete, assume you have savings of $70,000 in an account earning 2%.

Figure 9-1: Budget Gap Worsens with a Reverse Mortgage

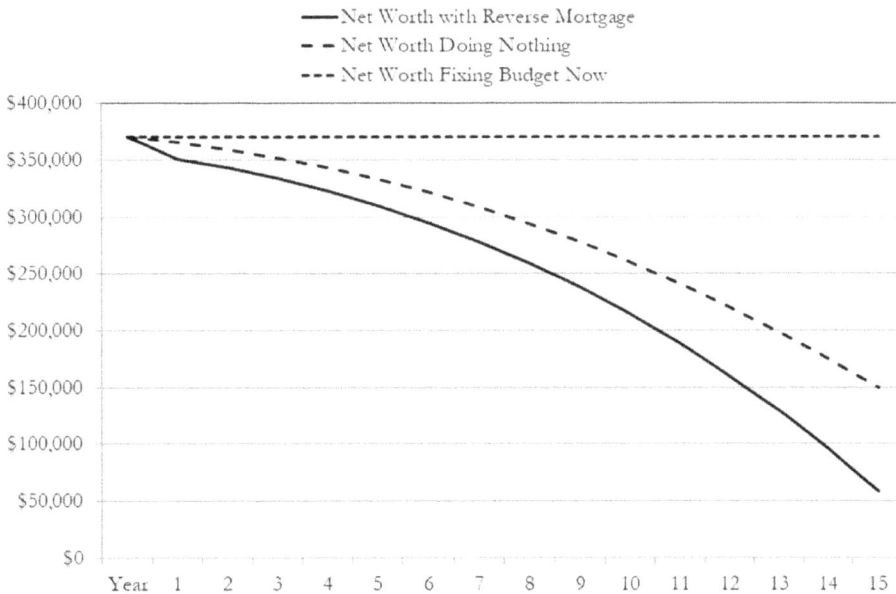

In these circumstances, tenure reverse mortgage payments of $620 monthly would fill the gap between income and expenses with $120 to spare at first. But time will pass and costs will rise. At only 2%, presently the

Federal Reserve's inflation target, it will take less than three years for expenses to once again surpass cash flow, inclusive of the reverse mortgage payments. You could then sell your home and get your expenses in line, but after paying off the reverse mortgage you will have about $51,000 less to work with.

If instead you remain in your home, even with the reverse mortgage cash payments you will run out of money in year 14. You will have to move at this point. But instead of getting $300,000 for your home, you will net less than $100,000 after paying around $200,000 to settle the reverse mortgage. Appreciation and additional cash from the reverse mortgage line of credit could extend your stay a little longer, but the added interest costs would only exacerbate your financial decline. Chapter 13 covers the topic of appreciation more fully.

What you should do instead

Your better route is to address your budget. Obviously, first seek ways to either reduce expenses or increase income. In the example above the target is $500.

If you have no avenue to close the gap alone, you could coordinate affairs with family, especially members who stand to inherit your home. Family circumstances would dictate the extent of formality needed; e.g. gifts versus loans with limited documentation versus arrangements with more structure.

Family members could also become party to a cosigned home equity loan or line of credit. Either would bring on debt, but at far less cost than a reverse mortgage. Saving your estate and financial legacy is worth a family discussion.

If you cannot close the gap and cannot coordinate with others, accept the fact that you should move. You cannot afford your current lifestyle. Adding the expense of a reverse mortgage will only make things worse. The cash offered is a teasing temporary band aid.

The exorbitant costs and ever-growing balance of a reverse mortgage will destroy your wealth and future options. Move now and use the full value of your home to buy or rent an affordable place. If you wait too long, you might find yourself literally impoverished – with no home equity and nothing in the bank due to the reverse mortgage.

10: Don't Get One to Improve Your Home

Reverse mortgage bankers would love to lend you money for home improvement purposes. The institution will either earn outsized fees for a temporary loan or garner vastly more in the long run, secured by a lien on your newly improved house.

Assume home and mortgage circumstances outlined in Appendix A. At age 65, you would be able to borrow a maximum of 43% of your home's $300,000 value, or $129,000. Net of closing costs, you would have access to $115,500 to improve your home.

Figure 10-1: Improve & Lose a Home with a Reverse Mortgage

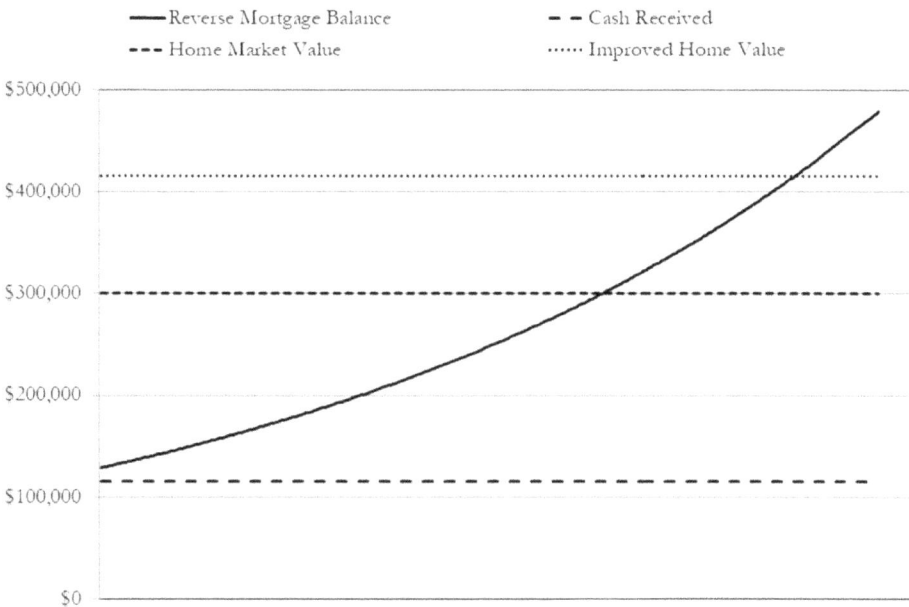

Legend: ── Reverse Mortgage Balance – – Cash Received --- Home Market Value ⋯⋯ Improved Home Value

While you did not receive a penny in cash, in about 15 years, your reverse mortgage balance will pass the original appraised $300,000 value of your home. If your improvements add value to your house dollar for dollar, your reverse mortgage balance will pass the enhanced home value only a few years later. Appreciation will not lessen the damage the loan does to your finances. Read Chapter 13.

From the bank's point of view you did not improve your home. You upgraded an investment property it controls via a lien. If you sell and move out after only a few years, you will have taken out and paid off an enormously expensive short-term loan. If you remain long enough, the bank will receive 95% of the proceeds from your home's sale. After transaction costs, you will get zilch. Since contractors doing the upgrades took the loan proceeds, effectively you gave away your home for nothing.

What you should do instead

If you want to make a major home improvement and can afford it, great. If you are not able to fund a home improvement through your own resources or a low-cost loan that gets paid off, you cannot afford that home improvement. You should not do it.

11: Don't Get One to Buy a Home

Going even further than home improvement, some firms present reverse mortgages as a tool to help finance a new home purchase. Make a deposit, pay nothing more, and somehow still own a home.

Assume circumstances outlined in Appendix A. At 65 you buy a $300,000 home and borrow as much as you can with a reverse mortgage. At 5%, your maximum initial balance is $129,000. After closing costs, the bank lends you $115,500. You pay the remaining $184,500 out of your own savings.

Figure 11-1: Reverse Mortgage Share of New Home Purchase

$300,000 Home, 65 Year-Old, 5% Interest, 20 Years

—— Reverse Mortgage Balance   --- Home Market Value   – – Cash Received

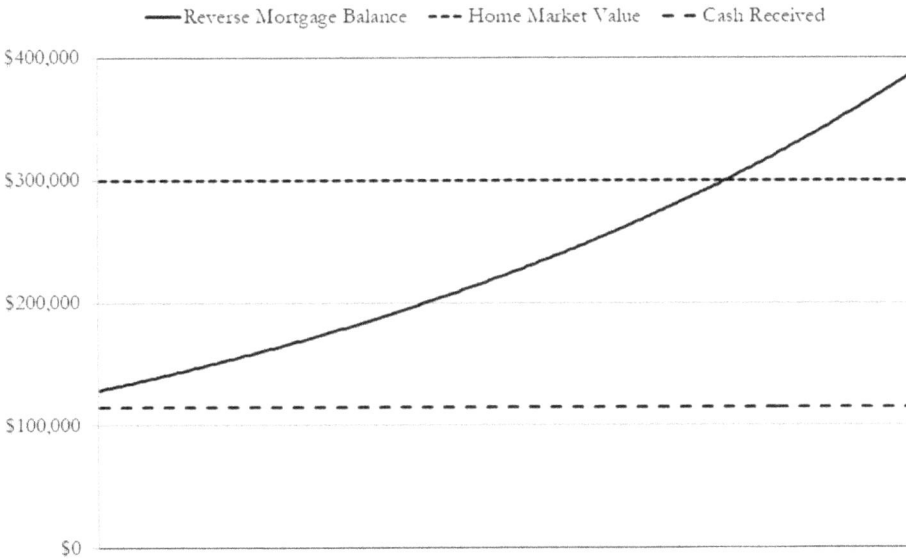

Going forward, you would not have to make any mortgage payments, but the mortgage balance will grow. In eight years you will owe more than $200,000; and seven years later the loan balance will surpass the original $300,000 home value. Appreciation does not lessen the financial damage of the loan; see Chapter 13.

Looked at from another angle, you pay $184,500 out of pocket up front; maintain the property; insure it; pay all taxes; and in the long run, net of transaction costs all proceeds from the property sale will go to the bank. Neither you nor your heirs will get a penny.

What you should do instead

If you can pay for a desired home outright or with a deposit and a conventional mortgage, go for it. Otherwise, accept the fact that you cannot afford it.

If you buy a home using a reverse mortgage, whatever home equity you acquire initially will be eaten up by the growing loan costs. In only a few years you would have neither home equity nor the liquid assets – the stocks, bonds, and cash – you sacrificed at closing. Don't do it.

12: Don't Get One to Delay Social Security

In another scheme aimed at gullible seniors, some firms push the notion of delaying Social Security until the full benefits can be reaped while using a reverse mortgage to get cash flow in the early years. They point to the cash. They hide the damage.

If you were born before 1959, you can receive full Social Security benefits if you start in the year you turn 66. You can instead choose to start receiving benefits when you are 62 years old, but you will receive 25% less.

If you do not need Social Security income between ages 62 and 65, your decision as to the starting date is simply a matter of your own desire.

For the moment, assume you need cash flow when you are 62, and that your full monthly benefit at age 66 is projected to be $2,500. At 62, you would only get $1,875 per month. For simplicity, assume no inflation and no further wages that would impact the payments. To fill out the picture, you own a $300,000 home and are considering a reverse mortgage with 5% interest.

Figure 12-1: Early Social Security vs. Reverse Mortgage Cash

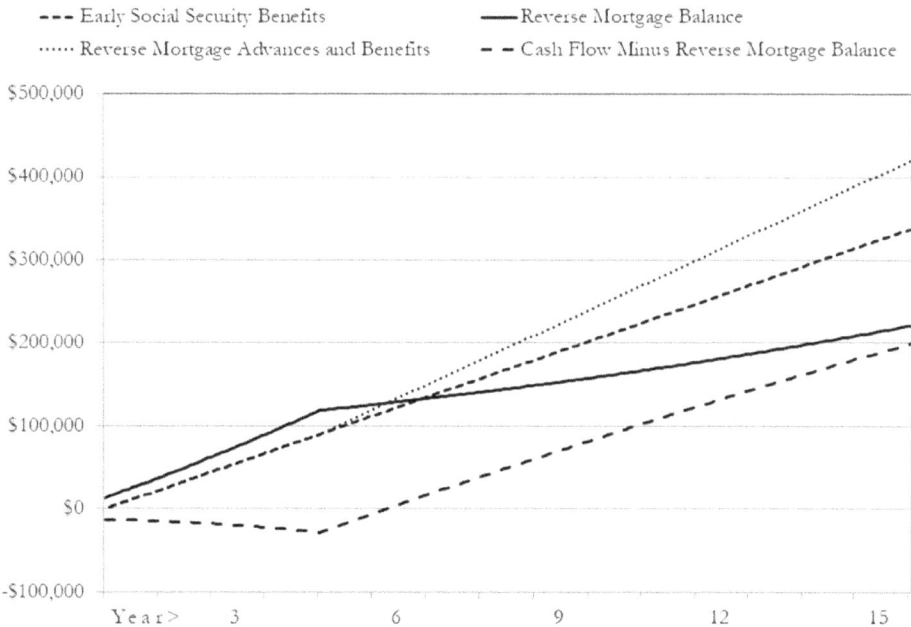

In the base case, you can simply start receiving Social Security benefits of $1,875 per month. After a year you will have received $22,500. After four years your accumulated benefit would be $90,000. In ten years you will have received $225,000. At all three points you still have complete, debtless ownership of your home.

In the alternate case, you delay Social Security benefits for four years and use a reverse mortgage to generate cash flow of $1,875 per month. After a year you will have received the same $22,500 as in the base case; but by borrowing everything, including the closing costs and interest you will owe the bank about $37,645. After four years your accumulated cash advances would be $90,000 – same as the early Social Security stream – but your debt would then be about $118,564.

At this point, at age 66, you would qualify for the full Social Security benefit of $2,500 per month. This would increase your cash flow by $625 per month. But in the same month you start receiving benefits, the interest and mortgage insurance on your reverse mortgage would add about $611 to your debt. As the balance grows, the interest and insurance will grow. In half a year you would lose more in interest and fees than the $625 you gained delaying benefits. This harm will grow for the rest of your life.

In ten years, with the reverse mortgage scenario, cumulative cash flow would amount to $270,000, a $45,000 improvement to the base case of taking Social Security early. But your debt will have ballooned to $166,921. Net, you would be worse off by over $120,000. In the 20th year, even though you would not have received a penny from the bank since that 4-year stretch from age 62 through 65, your loan balance will exceed your $300,000 home value. The bank will effectively own your house; you will have dumped it for total compensation of about $625 per month starting in your 66th year. Appreciation will not lessen the damage, as the next chapter explains.

What you should do instead

As mentioned earlier, if you do not need Social Security income to meet your living expenses, you can pick any starting date. The monthly amount you receive rises as you push the starting date out further. Sadly, but logically, when you wait longer, you will collect for fewer months. There are online calculators which can help you evaluate which stream makes the most sense.

If you need income that Social Security would provide and are 62 or above, you have a number of choices.

You can start collecting right away. Per above, this is vastly superior to borrowing.

You can work – or work more – and hold off the start of Social Security.

Even better in terms of cash flow, you could start collecting Social Security early and keep working. The more you work, the more you collect from Social Security. Benefit levels are adjusted annually both by inflation and via calculations involving your wage history. If you work more – even if you already started to collect – your benefits rise.

If you do not want to work and find early Social Security benefits inadequate, you have a budget gap. You should not worsen this gap and sacrifice your home equity with a reverse mortgage. You should address the gap now, gainfully. Read Chapter 9.

13: Appreciation Worsens Reverse Mortgage Harm

To isolate the effects of a reverse mortgage, most examples in this book far assume no home appreciation and no change in interest rates. A pushy rep might bring up home appreciation as a source of extra benefits that will offset the financial harm of a reverse mortgage. A rise in the market value of a home and the allowable maximum loan balance could lead to higher credit limits and additional cash flow.

However, more cash received is more cash owed. Net, when you factor in fees and interest your additional borrowing worsens your net worth.

Moreover, a rise in home prices would be a manifestation of inflation; and inflation – often merely the fear of inflation – brings higher interest rates. These higher rates will magnify the reverse mortgage harm as these rates apply to the entire balance, not just the new cash advances.

All term and tenure reverse mortgages have variable interest rates. So too do loans in which a line of credit is tapped after the first year. The only type of reverse mortgage with a fixed rate – a rate that would never go up or down – is a loan in which all money is taken as a lump sum in the first year. But if a lump sum borrower pulls out more cash any time after the first year, the rate will lose its fixed status and become variable, just like all other reverse mortgage types. Thus any scenario trying to demonstrate the benefit of extra cash from home price appreciation must also include the impact of higher rates.

Figure 13-1: Reverse Mortgage Harm with Inflation

As of:	Reverse Mortgage Balance	Cash Received	Home Value	Home plus Cash minus Mortgage
Closing	$129,000	$115,500	$300,000	$286,500
1 year	$144,453	$120,756	$312,222	$288,525
5 years	$221,722	$144,009	$366,299	$288,585
10 years	$364,044	$178,817	$447,250	$262,024
15 years	$580,120	$221,319	$546,090	$187,290

Importantly, interest rates as of this writing are still near historic lows; which means the examples in this book are basically best-case scenarios. Introduce an environment with inflation and rising interest rates, the magnitude of reverse mortgage damage explodes.

To demonstrate, assume circumstances outlined in Appendix A. But in this scenario also assume annual home appreciation of 4% and interest rates that are higher by 2%, only half the inflation amount. This would cause the initial 5% interest rate to rise to 7%.

As a 65-year-old with a $300,000 home, at 5% your maximum initial balance would be $129,000. Net of closing costs about $115,500 would be available. With appreciation, your rising home value multiplied by the H.U.D. percentage limit can render higher maximum lending amounts. Assume a loan-friendly scenario in which appreciation is instantly reflected in your home value, allowing you to take out the maximum allowed monthly.

Under these circumstances, one year out you will have received an extra $5,260, bringing your amount received to $120,726. You will owe $144,453. As of the end of year five, you will have received total payments of $144,009; you will owe $221,721. In year ten, cumulative cash received will hit $178,817; you will owe $364,044.

Figure 13-2: Reverse Mortgage Harm with Inflation

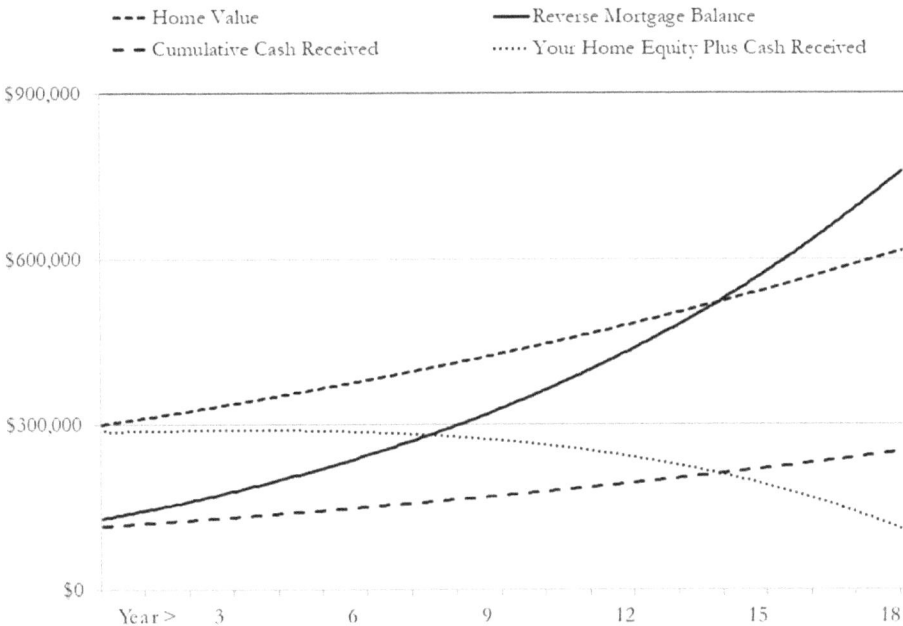

Put another way, without the reverse mortgage in year ten you would own your appreciated house free and clear at a value of $447,500. With the reverse mortgage, your home equity would be less than $84,000. You threw away $364,044 in return for less than half that amount in cash. As time passes, it only gets worse.

Without appreciation and new borrowings, the reverse mortgage balance approaches home value in about 16 years. With 4% appreciation and only a 2% increase in rates, the mortgage balance approaches home value in about 14 years.

Historically, interest rates usually rise in lockstep with inflation, not at half the pace, so this scenario above is very generous to the reverse mortgage case. Whether using these generous assumptions or more realistic ones with even higher rates, debt will rise by an astonishingly higher amount than the extra cash received.

As explained throughout this book, reverse mortgages are horribly damaging in a stagnant, low interest rate environment. With appreciation, inflation, and higher rates, they are even worse.

14: A Societal Case against Reverse Mortgages

Personal finance aside, there is an important societal reason why reverse mortgages deserve to be fully exposed and rejected. It is not news that we Americans are terrible savers. Whether out of necessity or overindulgence, we tend to spend what we make. The median American has nothing set aside for retirement. Among the 48% of adults who have retirement accounts, as of this edition the average level of savings is under $100,000, perhaps a few years of expenses if carefully managed.

Figure 14-1: Median Household Assets 1989-2013

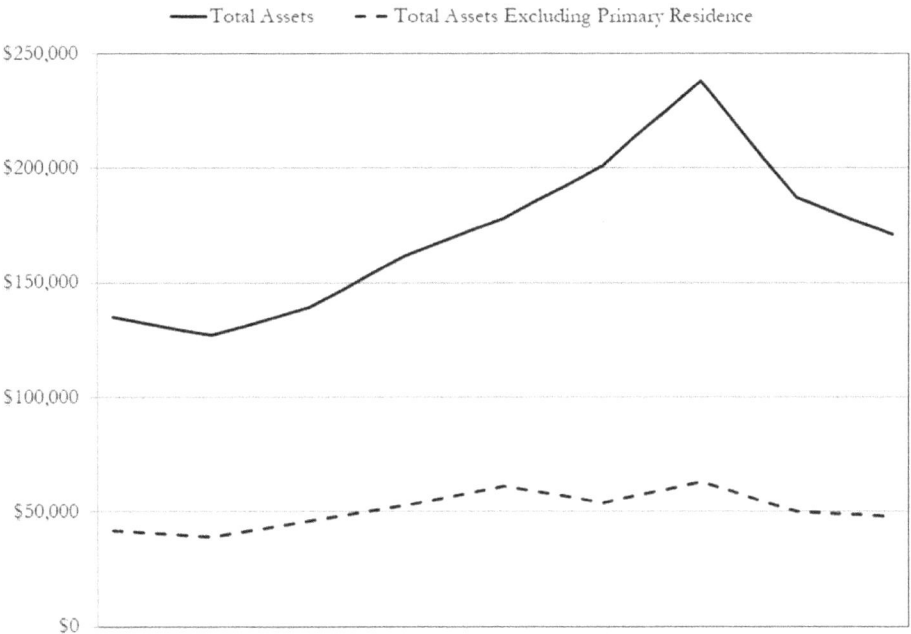

A major reason working- and middle-class families have been able to grow wealth in succeeding generations is the stored and thankfully illiquid savings found in home ownership. Unable to spend 'house', as time passes families grow wealth through their home equity. For the median household, equity value in a home has consistently represented between two and three times the value of all other assets combined. The discipline of paying down mortgages, taking care of a property, and ultimately selling at full value or handing it over to heirs has been a bedrock of generational growth in middle class living standards.

Reverse mortgages threaten to stop this secular improvement in one sweeping blow.

Conclusion

In their current form, reverse mortgages are a travesty. Their financially malicious nature is obvious to anyone who understands the math.

As stated and mathematically demonstrated, in the short run reverse mortgage costs are more egregious than the vig charged by criminal loan sharks. In the long run, reverse mortgages transfer effective ownership of your home to the bank for a fraction of its value.

Don't bring on debt to spend on unneeded things. If you cannot afford your living expenses, be smart: get a home equity loan or line of credit; temporarily use a credit card; budget better; make arrangements with family; move.

Do anything but a reverse mortgage. Anything is better.

Appendices

Appendix A: Lump Sum Reverse Mortgage
Appendix B: Term Reverse Mortgage
Appendix C: Tenure Reverse Mortgage
Appendix D: H.U.D. Factors / Fire Sale Discount

Appendix A: Lump Sum Reverse Mortgage

A Simplified Example for Demonstration

Assumptions and Terms:

Age of youngest borrower: 65
Assessed home value: $300,000
Interest rate: 5% (fixed)
Percentage limit of beginning loan balance (from H.U.D.): 43%
Maximum beginning loan balance (43% of $300,000): $129,000
Mortgage insurance due at closing: $6,000
Origination fee: $5,000
Other closing costs (estimate): $2,500
Total closing costs: $13,500
Net cash available: $115,500
Continuing mortgage insurance: 0.5% per year

A 65 year-old homeowner borrowing through a reverse mortgage at an interest rate of 5% could get approval for an initial loan amount equal to 43% of the appraised home value, at most. Assuming a home value of $300,000, the maximum initial balance would be $129,000. Closing costs in line with industry norms and H.U.D guidelines would be about $13,500. Subtracting these costs from the maximum initial balance, upon closing a net figure of $115,500 woud be available to the borrower.

Figure A-1: Reverse Mortgage - Lump Sum Option

When	New Cash Received	Cumulative Cash Received	Reverse Mortgage Loan Balance	Your Home Equity Plus Cash Received
Before Closing				$300,000
Upon Closing	$115,500	$115,500	$129,000	$286,500
Year 1	$0	$115,500	$136,277	$279,223
Year 2	$0	$115,500	$143,964	$271,536
Year 3	$0	$115,500	$152,084	$263,416
Year 4	$0	$115,500	$160,663	$254,837
Year 5	$0	$115,500	$169,726	$245,774
Years 6-10	$0	$115,500	$223,309	$192,191
Years 11-15	$0	$115,500	$293,808	$121,692
Years 16-20	$0	$115,500	$386,565	$28,935
Years 21-25	$0	$115,500	$508,605	-$93,105

Going forward, interest of 5% plus mortgage insurance of 0.5% would be charged, rendering a nominal total rate of 5.5% applied to the outstanding balance. Importantly, this is not the effective annual percentage rate (APR). Because of the enormous closing costs, the APR on a lump sum reverse mortgages is vastly higher than the quoted interest rate.

Figures A-1 and A-2 show amounts received and owed over time. Also shown is the sum of the homeowner's share of the home equity plus cash received from the reverse mortgage.

Figure A-2: Reverse Mortgage - Lump Sum Option

——Reverse Mortgage Loan Balance
– – Cumulative Cash Received
--- Your Home Equity Plus Cash Received

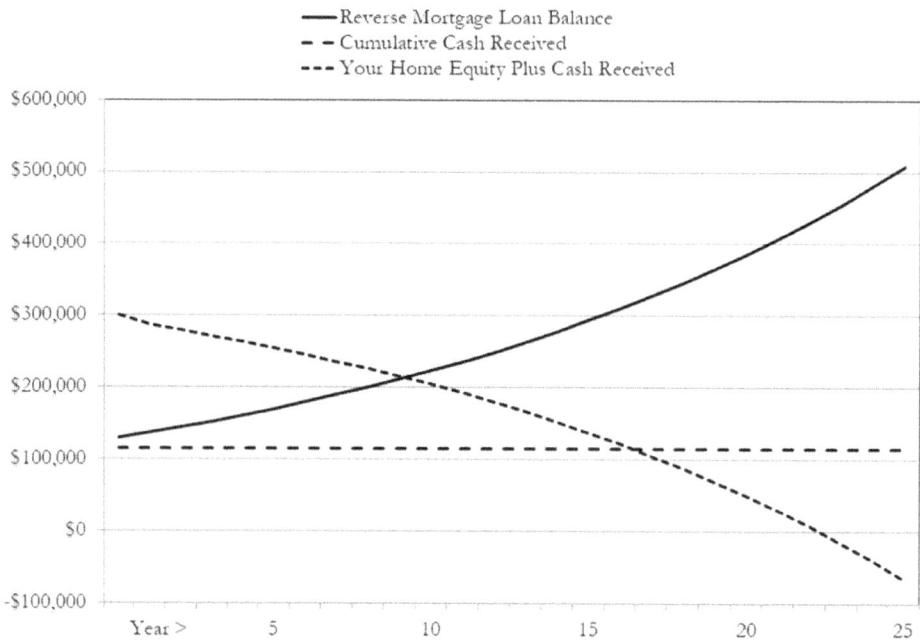

Before the loan, the borrower owns all $300,000 worth of the home. Upon receiving $115,500, the borrower owes $129,000 to the bank. The bank in turn has a claim of $129,000 on the house, which leaves the borrower with $171,000 in home equity. Adding this remaining home equity to the $115,500 cash received renders total assets related to the home equal to $286,500. The borrower worsened his/her overall wealth by $13,500.

After five years, the loan balance will be $169,726. The borrower's home equity will be down to $130,274. Adding back the cash received, total home related assets will be down to $245,774. The borrower will have thown away $54,226 through the reverse mortgage.

After ten years, the loan balance hits $223,309, almost double the cash received. After 15 years, the balance owed reaches $293,808, practically the entire original equity of of the home. As transaction costs of selling a home can easily exceed 5% of the home value, a borrower has effectively lost all the original home equity after 15 years. In this case the home owner lost $300,000, dumping the equity for $115,500 in cash. Appreciation will not help. See Chapter 13.

As for the aforementioned APR, the actual effective annual percentage cost of any reverse mortgage will not be known until the loan is paid off. While the closing costs are known, the amount borrowed can vary and the date when the loan will be paid off is not known. But the APR can be shown for any possible combination of amounts and dates.

Figure A-3 displays APRs for the loan modeled in this appendix (5% nominal rate, $300,000 home value, 65-year old borrower) and various borrowing levels and payoff dates. For reference, conventional mortgage rates were less than 4% at the time of this writing.

Figure A-3: Effective APR - Lump Sum Option

Time When Loan Is Paid Off	Borrow the Maximum	Borrow 75% of the Maximum	Borrow 50% of the Maximum
End of Year 1	17.99%	57.32%	135.98%
End of Year 2	11.64%	28.92%	57.89%
End of Year 3	9.61%	20.64%	38.09%
End of Year 4	8.60%	16.70%	29.15%
End of Year 5	8.00%	14.40%	24.06%
End of Year 10	6.75%	9.87%	14.41%
End of Year 15	6.34%	8.40%	11.37%

Commercials for reverse mortgages highlight the fact that one can borrow as much – up to the legal maximum – or as little as one wants. Most of the examples in this book assume maximal borrowings, which are best case scenarios in terms of the cost of money. Figure A-3 highlights the mathematical fact that the APR is worse when less is borrowed.

Ads also emphasize the ability to pay off the loan whenever one wants. But when paid off in the first few years, the APR rises to usurious levels. Of course, if held for a long time, a borrower will effectively lose all the home equity. A lump sum reverse mortgages is a lose-lose proposition.

Appendix B: Term Reverse Mortgage

A Simplified Example for Demonstration

Assumptions and Terms:

Age of youngest borrower: 65
Assessed home value: $300,000
Interest rate: 5% (variable…but herein assume no changes)
Percentage limit of beginning loan balance: 43%
Maximum present value of loan (43% of $300,000): $129,000
Mortgage insurance due at closing: $6,000
Origination fee: $5,000
Other closing costs (estimate): $2,500
Total closing costs: $13,500
Maximum present value of monthly payments: $115,500
Monthly payments for a term of 20 years: $794.51
Continuing mortgage insurance: 0.5% per year
Monthly service fee: $25

A 65 year-old homeowner borrowing through a reverse mortgage at an interest rate of 5% could get approval for monthly payments which would have a present value worth, at most, 43% of the home value minus closing costs. Assuming a home value of $300,000, a calculated maximum level of $129,000, closing costs of $13,500, and a 20-year term, monthly payments for those 20 years would be about $795.

Figure B-1: Reverse Mortgage - Term Option

When	New Cash Received	Cumulative Cash Received	Reverse Mortgage Balance	Home Equity Plus Cash Received
Before Closing				$300,000
Upon Closing	$0	$0	$13,500	$286,500
Year 1	$9,534	$9,534	$24,347	$285,187
Year 2	$9,534	$19,068	$35,807	$283,262
Year 3	$9,534	$28,602	$47,912	$280,690
Year 4	$9,534	$38,136	$60,701	$277,436
Year 5	$9,534	$47,671	$74,211	$273,460
Years 6-10	$47,671	$95,341	$154,088	$241,254
Years 11-15	$47,671	$143,012	$259,182	$183,830
Years 16-20	$47,671	$190,682	$397,455	$93,227
Years 21-25	$0	$190,682	$522,934	-$32,251

Going forward, interest plus mortgage insurance of 0.5% would be charged. Generously assuming the variable rate remains at 5%, a total nominal annual rate of 5.5% would be applied to the outstanding balance. Just as with the lump sum option, this is not the effective annual percentage rate (APR). Because of the huge closing costs, the APR on a term reverse mortgage is much higher than the quoted interest rate. Also, with a monthly payment option, each payment would incur a service charge as high as $30. For this scenario assume a charge of $25. Figures B-1 and B-2 show amounts received and owed over time using the assumptions above.

Before the loan, the $300,000 home is owned free and clear. As of closing and the first payment, the borrower would receive $795. The bank would be owed $14,295, equal to the payment plus closing costs. Going forward the borrower would receive about $795 each month while the loan balance would increase by that same $795 plus the $25 service fee plus interest and mortgage insurance on the balance carried from the previous month.

Figure B-2: Reverse Mortgage - Term Option

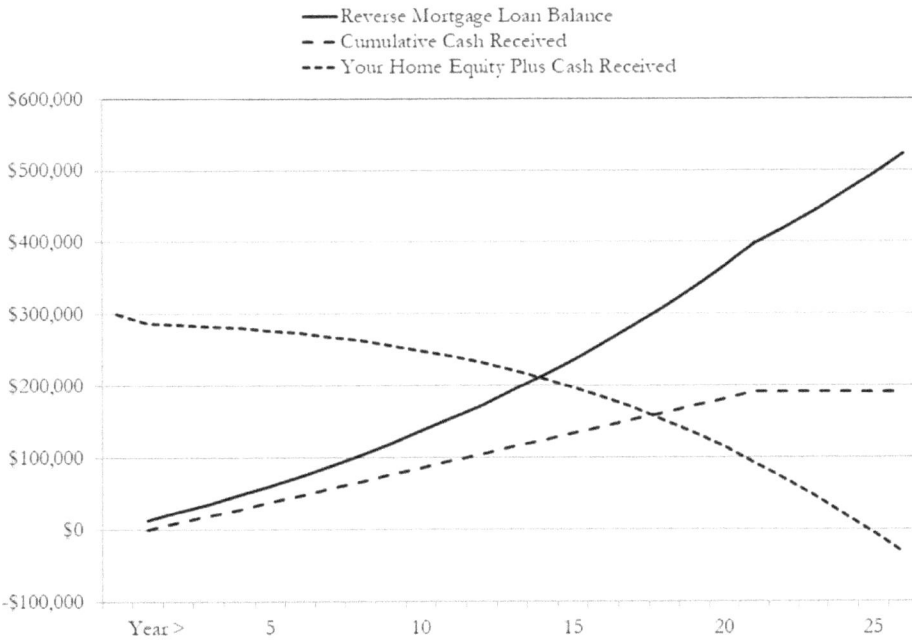

— Reverse Mortgage Loan Balance
— — Cumulative Cash Received
--- Your Home Equity Plus Cash Received

By the end of the first year a total of $9,534 will have been paid to the borrower. The bank will be owed $24,347. After ten years $95,341 will have been paid to the borrower; the bank's claim upon the house will be up to $154,088. Adding the cash received to the remaining home equity, total assets related to the house sum to $241,254. The reverse mortgage caused a loss in net worth of almost $60,000; so far.

At the end of the term, $190,682 will have been received. $397,455 will be owed. A bank cannot collect more than 95% of a home's value upon sale or foreclosure; transaction costs easily take up the remaining 5%. It is nonetheless clear that by the end of the term the borrower's equity is long gone. Upon sale, foreclosure, or inheritance, not a penny will go to the borrower or his/her heirs. $190,682 received over time was the compensation. In present value terms, the home was sold for $115,500.

As mentioned in Appendix A, the APR, the effective annual percentage rate, will not be known ahead of time because the actual cash flow, incoming and out, are not set. Figure B-3 displays APRs for the term loan modeled in this appendix with various borrowing levels and payoff dates.

Figure B-3: Effective APR - Term Option

Time When Loan Is Paid Off	Borrow the Maximum	Borrow 75% of the Maximum	Borrow 50% of the Maximum
End of Year 1	487.00%	837.92%	1651.45%
End of Year 2	81.57%	131.27%	218.26%
End of Year 3	38.62%	63.28%	102.50%
End of Year 4	24.71%	41.13%	65.98%
End of Year 5	18.31%	30.64%	48.77%
End of Year 10	9.23%	14.71%	22.33%
End of Year 15	7.39%	10.86%	15.62%

Ads for reverse mortgages highlight the fact that one can borrow as little as one wants and pay off the loan whenever one wants. Figure B-3 shows that when the term loan is utilized to the fullest, it has high cost. If less is borrowed or if the loan is paid off early, its cost is astronomical.

Keep in mind the above scenario assumes a fairly best case scenario of constant interest rates set in a time of record low rates. Conventional mortgage rates were less than 4% at the time of this writing. If rates rise, the damage to family finances of a term reverse mortgage will be far worse.

Appendix C: Tenure Reverse Mortgage

A Simplified Example for Demonstration

Assumptions and Terms:

Age of youngest borrower: 65
Assessed home value: $300,000
Interest rate: 5% (variable…but herein assume no changes)
Percentage limit of beginning loan balance: 43%
Maximum present value of loan (43% times $300,000): $129,000
Mortgage insurance due at closing: $6,000
Origination fee: $5,000
Other closing costs (estimate): $2,500
Total closing costs: $13,500
Maximum present value of monthly payments: $115,500
Monthly payments for life: $620.25
Continuing mortgage insurance: 0.5% per year
Monthly service fee: $25

A 65 year-old homeowner borrowing through a reverse mortgage at an interest rate of 5% could get approval for monthly payments which would have a present value worth, at most, 43% of the home value minus closing costs. Assuming a home value of $300,000, a calculated maximum level of $129,000, and closing costs of $13,500, the monthly payments would be about $620 for life.

Figure C-1: Reverse Mortgage - Tenure Option

When	New Cash Received	Cumulative Cash Received	Reverse Mortgage Balance	Home Equity Plus Cash Received
Before Closing				$300,000
Upon Closing	$0	$0	$13,500	$286,500
Year 1	$7,443	$7,443	$22,203	$285,240
Year 2	$7,443	$14,886	$31,396	$283,490
Year 3	$7,443	$22,329	$41,109	$281,220
Year 4	$7,443	$29,772	$51,369	$278,403
Year 5	$7,443	$37,215	$62,208	$275,008
Years 6-10	$37,215	$74,430	$126,292	$248,138
Years 11-15	$37,215	$111,646	$210,609	$201,037
Years 16-20	$37,215	$148,861	$321,545	$127,316
Years 21-25	$37,215	$186,076	$467,503	$18,573

Going forward, interest plus mortgage insurance of 0.5% would be charged. Generously assuming the variable rate remains at 5%, a total annual rate of 5.5% would be applied to the outstanding balance. Just as with the other payment options, this is not the effective annual percentage rate (APR). Because of the massive closing costs, the APR on a tenure reverse mortgage is much higher than the quoted interest rate. Also, each payment would incur a service charge as high as $30. For this scenario assume a fee of $25. Figures C-1 and C-2 show amounts received and owed over time using these assumptions.

Before the loan, the $300,000 home is owned free and clear. As of closing and the first payment, the borrower would receive $620. The bank would be owed $14,120, equal to the payment plus closing costs. Going forward the borrower would receive $620 each month while the loan balance would increase by that same $620 plus the $25 service fee plus interest and mortgage insurance on the balance carried from the previous month.

By the end of the first year a total of $7,443 will have been paid to the borrower. The bank will be owed, and have a claim upon the house of $22,203. The borrower's home equity will be down to $277,797. Adding this to the cash received, the total of home related assets is $285,240, a drop in net worth of almost $15,000.

Figure C-2: Reverse Mortgage - Tenure Option

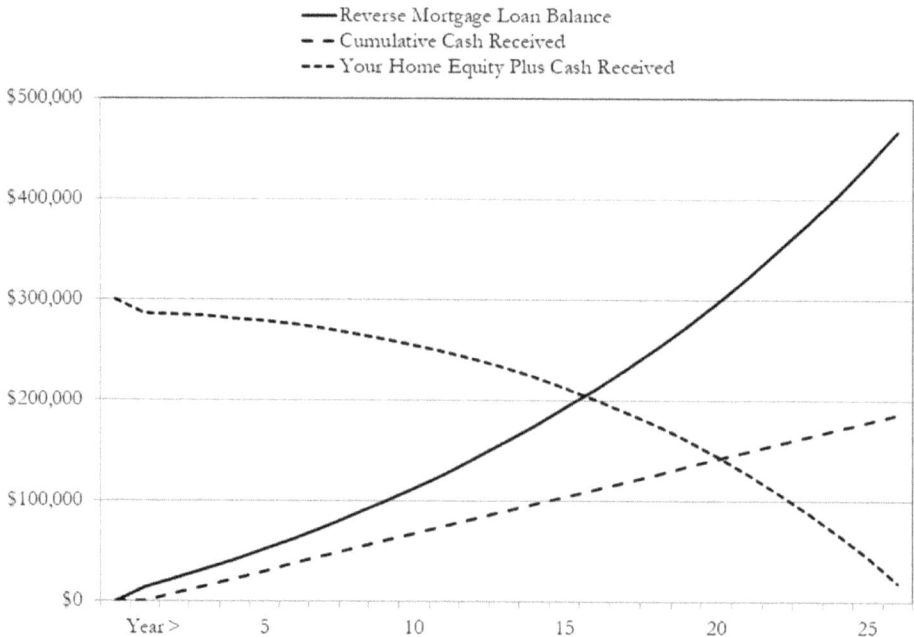

——Reverse Mortgage Loan Balance
– – Cumulative Cash Received
- - - Your Home Equity Plus Cash Received

At the end of ten years, $74,430 will have been paid to the borrower. The bank's claim upon the house will be up to $126,292, rendering net harm of roughly $52,000. As of the end of year 20, the loan balance will hit $321,545 while the borrower will have received only $148,861. Put another way, the borrower will have received less than half the appraised value of the home and yet will owe the bank more than that original value. In present value terms, of course, the borrower traded away the entire home equity for $115,500.

As with the lump sum and term options, the APR, the effective annual percentage rate – the true cost of the loan – will not be known until the loan is paid off. Figure C-3 shows APRs for the tenure loan modeled in this appendix with various borrowing levels and payoff dates.

Figure C-3: Effective APR - Tenure Option

Time When Loan Is Paid Off	Borrow the Maximum	Borrow 75% of the Maximum	Borrow 50% of the Maximum
End of Year 1	658.38%	1096.81%	2105.26%
End of Year 2	100.56%	154.01%	247.44%
End of Year 3	46.45%	71.93%	112.47%
End of Year 4	29.22%	45.90%	71.20%
End of Year 5	21.32%	33.75%	52.06%
End of Year 10	10.00%	15.47%	23.08%
End of Year 15	7.65%	11.11%	15.86%

As mentioned before, reverse mortgage purveyors emphasize the fact that one can borrow pretty much any amount up to the maximum, and pay off the loan whenever one chooses. Figure C-3 shows that when the tenure loan is tapped to its maximum level, it is extremely costly – moreso than the lump sum and term options. If one borrows less or pays the loan off early, the cost is absolutely absurd.

Again, the above scenario assumes a fairly best case of constant interest rates in a time of record low rates. If rates rise, the damage to family finances of a tenure reverse mortgage would be even more devastating.

Appendix D: H.U.D. Factors / Fire Sale Discount

The factors in Figures D-1 and D-2, from H.U.D. as of this writing, show the maximum percent of home value you can be approved for when you borrow through a reverse mortgage. Closing costs reduce this amount by several percent.

For example, at 5% a 65-year old could be approved for a loan in an amount equal to 43% of home value. If closing costs were 4.5% of home value, the borrower would get 38.5% of the home value, at most.

Figure D-1: H.U.D. Factors - Age 62 to 80

Age	Interest Rate					
	5%	6%	7%	8%	9%	10%
62	41.0%	35.7%	31.2%	27.2%	23.8%	20.9%
63	41.6%	36.4%	31.9%	27.9%	24.5%	21.5%
64	42.3%	37.1%	32.6%	28.6%	25.2%	22.2%
65	43.0%	37.8%	33.3%	29.4%	25.9%	22.9%
66	43.8%	38.6%	34.1%	30.1%	26.7%	23.6%
67	44.5%	39.4%	34.9%	30.9%	27.4%	24.4%
68	45.3%	40.2%	35.7%	31.7%	28.2%	25.2%
69	46.1%	41.0%	36.5%	32.6%	29.1%	26.0%
70	46.5%	41.5%	37.0%	33.0%	29.6%	26.5%
71	46.5%	41.5%	37.0%	33.1%	29.6%	26.5%
72	46.7%	41.6%	37.2%	33.2%	29.8%	26.7%
73	47.5%	42.5%	38.1%	34.2%	30.7%	27.6%
74	48.3%	43.4%	39.0%	35.0%	31.5%	28.4%
75	49.2%	44.3%	40.0%	36.0%	32.6%	29.4%
76	49.8%	45.0%	40.6%	36.7%	33.2%	30.1%
77	50.8%	46.0%	41.7%	37.8%	34.3%	31.2%
78	51.8%	47.1%	42.8%	38.9%	35.5%	32.4%
79	52.3%	47.7%	43.4%	39.6%	36.1%	33.0%
80	53.4%	48.8%	44.6%	40.8%	37.4%	34.2%

Explaining the notion of a 'fire sale discount', assume the 65-year old takes the full 38.5% in cash. The bank will be owed 43% of home value upon closing. Over time, the borrower receives nothing more. Meanwhile the bank's share of the home equity will rise from 43% to 95%.

Legally, a reverse mortgage lender cannot collect more than 95% of a home's value. The 5% margin is intended to cover transaction costs, such as one would incur if the home was sold or financed anew.

Banks do not want your house. They want the money from the loan's payoff. In the long run, a reverse mortgage lender will effectively get all the net proceeds from your home's sale. In the example just cited, you sold it for 38.5% of its value – a 61.5% fire sale discount.

Figure D-2: H.U.D. Factors - Age 81 to 99

Age	Interest Rate					
	5%	6%	7%	8%	9%	10%
81	54.5%	49.9%	45.8%	42.1%	38.7%	35.6%
82	55.6%	51.1%	47.1%	43.4%	40.0%	36.9%
83	56.7%	52.4%	48.4%	44.7%	41.4%	38.3%
84	57.9%	53.6%	49.7%	46.1%	42.8%	39.8%
85	59.1%	54.9%	51.1%	47.6%	44.4%	41.4%
86	60.3%	56.3%	52.6%	49.1%	45.9%	43.0%
87	61.6%	57.7%	54.0%	50.7%	47.6%	44.7%
88	62.6%	58.9%	55.3%	52.0%	49.0%	46.1%
89	64.0%	60.3%	56.9%	53.7%	50.8%	48.0%
90	65.3%	61.8%	58.6%	55.5%	52.6%	49.9%
91	66.7%	63.4%	60.3%	57.3%	54.6%	51.9%
92	68.2%	65.0%	62.0%	59.2%	56.6%	54.0%
93	69.7%	66.7%	63.9%	61.2%	58.7%	56.3%
94	71.2%	68.4%	65.8%	63.3%	60.9%	58.6%
95	72.7%	70.1%	67.6%	65.3%	63.0%	60.9%
96	73.4%	71.0%	68.6%	66.3%	64.1%	62.0%
97	74.0%	71.6%	69.3%	67.1%	65.0%	62.9%
98	74.0%	71.6%	69.3%	67.1%	65.0%	62.9%
99	74.0%	71.6%	69.3%	67.1%	65.0%	62.9%

Appendix E: List of Figures

About the Author

Art Ernst has been analyzing financial products for almost four decades. He has been writing about them for about three decades.

Art earned his M.B.A. at the Wharton Graduate School of Business in 1984 and was the 1981 recipient of the Eugene E. Agger Memorial Award as the top economics graduate at Rutgers College. He began his career on Wall Street directing projects involved with every phase of development of financial products including funds, annuities, loans and retirement plans. Since 1984 he has managed portfolios for individuals and institutions including mutual funds, insurance companies and foundations.

When Art's children were young he formed an independent consultancy to manage affairs in a family-friendly manner. During this period, he shopped for financial services as a regular consumer. This new perspective changed everything. He resolved to address the sales gimmicks, excessive fees, imprudence, and scams he encountered as a 'retail' financial customer.

Additional to his service on behalf of investment management and financial planning clients, Art has written educational pieces to help the public at large avoid common wealth-harming Wall Street tactics. His articles have been published in several journals, magazines and newspapers. He is the author of "A Consumer's Guide to Harmful Investment Products" and "A Consumer's Guide to Harmful Financial Products".

A Registered Investment Advisor first licensed in 1982, Art is a portfolio manager and the Chief Operating Officer at Byrne Asset Management LLC in Princeton, New Jersey.

www.ingramcontent.com/pod-product-compliance
Lightning Source LLC
Chambersburg PA
CBHW051425200326
41520CB00023B/7356